To: _____

_____

From: _____

_____

For all God's children with the prayer that through His inspiration we may better serve mankind.

Inspirations From the Heart
art copyright © 1997 by P. Buckley Moss
copyright © 1997 by Landauer Books,
a division of Landauer Corporation,
12251 Maffitt Road, Cumming, Iowa 50061

President and Publisher: Jeramy Lanigan Landauer
Editor: Becky Johnston
Art Director: Lyne Neymeyer
Graphic Designer: Nicole Bratt
Prepress: Event Graphics
Printed in Mexico

This book is printed on acid-free paper.

ISBN: 0964-6870-7-0

10 9 8 7 6 5 4 3 2 1
First Edition

Other books in this series:
A Journal From the Heart
An Address Book From the Heart

P Buckley Moss®

LANDAUER BOOKS
LANDAUER CORPORATION
CUMMING, IOWA

The Artist

P. Buckley Moss, one of America's most celebrated artists, is a phenomenon: in her gifts and imagery, her popularity, and in her ability to communicate on many levels to many people.

P. Buckley Moss is also well-known for her work with special education groups and her generous donations to charity. Primarily because of her dyslexia and childhood struggles, Pat Moss has become a role model to the learning impaired and has raised millions of dollars for children's charities.

Assisting her in these efforts is the P. Buckley Moss Society with 60 chapters and more than 20,000 members.

The Art of P. Buckley Moss

P. Buckley Moss is an artist of friendly images that radiate significant messages. She is a master at projecting positive impressions full of feeling, memory, and hope. With a few well-chosen graceful lines and a limited amount of color, her art communicates a philosophy based on faith and confident optimism.

Words reinforce for the mind what the eye sees. The words and the images chosen for this volume blend the beauty of the visual with the magnificence of language. *Inspirations From the Heart* is an aesthetic declaration of truths which our souls invariably remember. It is the familiar echo of the best of our inner selves.

Peter M. Rippe, Director
P. Buckley Moss Museum

Featured Plates

In Order of Appearance:

Apple Blossom Love (Cover), IS: 12¾" x 12¼", 1996

Just for Nana, IS: 7¼" x 4½", 1995

Shenandoah Memories, IS: 16⅛" x 17⅜", 1993

First Picnic, IS: 12½" x 12¾", 1985

Tender Shepherd, IS: 9½" x 9½", 1983

Our Teacher, IS: 12⅛" x 12³⁄₁₆", 1992

Never Ending Love, IS: 8" x 9⅛", 1995

Love in Bloom, IS: 11¼" x 11⅞", 1995

Summer's Blessing, IS: 7¾" x 8¾", 1985

Give Thanks, IS: 9" x 9", 1993

Christmas Carol, IS: 8" x 8", 1983

Stars of Love, IS: 12¾" x 11⁷⁄₁₆", 1993

Apple Blossom Love, IS: 12¾" x 12¼", 1996

Golden Autumn, IS: 17" x 17½", 1983

* All verse by Malcolm Henderson, except as noted.

For further information regarding P. Buckley Moss limited edition prints and original paintings, and for the name of the authorized dealer nearest you, please call The Moss Portfolio at 800/430-1320.

Introduction

Just as the seasons come and go, so do the familiar faces of those we hold so dear.

Knowing not what the future holds, we often fail to find ways to express our appreciation until the time for sharing has all too quickly passed.

It is my hope and desire that within these pages you'll find sentiments to share— expressions of love and gratitude for a special person, place or time. Or, perhaps a simple tribute to someone you hold in deep regard.

Most of all, may they be inspirations... from the heart!

Becky Johnston, Editor

'Tis a gift to be simple,
'Tis a gift to be free,
'Tis a gift to come down where we ought to be,
And when we find ourselves in the place just right,
'Twill be in the valley of love and delight.

Shaker Hymntune

Love Warms in Winter

...the lark is so brimful of gladness and love,
The green fields below him, the blue sky above,
That he sings, and he sings; for ever sings he—
"I love my Love, and my Love loves me!"

Samuel Taylor Coleridge

Love Blossoms in Spring

She walks—the lady of my delight—
A shepherdess of sheep.
Her flocks are thoughts, she keeps them white;
she guards them from the steep.
She feeds them on the fragrant height,
and folds them in for sleep.

Alice Meynell

Love Celebrates in Summer

Throughout our lives, we hold in deep regard
Those who've helped us to succeed.
And, how often it seems to be,
Our teacher is the one who cared and shared—
but most of all believed.

Love Mellows in Autumn

ABCDEFGHIJKLM
NOPQRSTUVWXYZ

First to last each other treasure,
Sharing always love's full measure.
Our hearts, our hopes, our joys, our tears
Mark the passage of our years.

Love Warms in Winter

In times of joy and times of need
A friend is always there—
Someone to share,
Someone to care;
A tender heart has love to spare!

Love Blossoms in Spring

All are but parts
of one stupendous whole,
Whose body Nature is,
and God the soul.

Alexander Pope

Love Celebrates in Summer

For health and food,
For love and friends,
For everything Thy goodness sends...
We thank Thee.

Ralph Waldo Emerson

Love Mellows in Autumn

And all the souls on earth shall sing
on Christmas day, on Christmas day;
And all the souls on earth shall sing
on Christmas day, in the morning.

Unknown

Love Warms in Winter

Quilted love so warm and true,
Reflections of my love for you!

Love Blossoms in Spring

My heart is like an apple-tree
Whose boughs are bent with thickset fruit;
My heart is like a rainbow shell
That paddles in a halcyon sea;
My heart is gladder than all these
Because my love is come to me.

Christina Georgina Rossetti

Love Celebrates in Summer

Please God, just as we treasure the golden moments
At the close of the day,
let us rejoice in the richest season of our lives—
when love mellows in Autumn.

Love Mellows in Autumn

*What lies behind us, and what lies before us
are tiny matters, compared to what lies within us.*

Ralph Waldo Emerson